Fairness

or
Folly

Published by:
Lindsey & Waldo, LLC
1050 Hillcrest Rd., Ste A
Mobile, AL 36695
Phone 251-633-4070
Fax 251-633-4071
www.CPAMobileAL.com

Printed by:
CreateSpace, An Amazon Company

Fairness

or

Folly

A Real World Guide
to the Temporary Tax Reform
of the Tax Cuts and Jobs Act

Richard A. Lindsey, CPA

Table of Contents

Confessions of a CPA

"The hardest thing in the world to understand is the income tax."
– Albert Einstein

I'm in favor of a balanced federal budget. I believe that continuing to increase our federal deficit can eventually bring financial ruin to our economy, our country, our entire way of life. The government cannot, no more than we can, spend its way out of debt. But, it is not your job, your obligation, or your responsibility, to pay down Uncle Sam's debt. Never has been.

Your responsibility is to pay your "fair" share as dictated by the tax laws of our country and not a penny more. But, there are conflicting rules and you can't take advantage of the tax rules to minimize your taxes unless you know what those rules are. And Congress and the IRS keep changing them on you, don't they? It's like they don't want you to be able to learn them and be done. Remember when you took European History, or Algebra, in school, once you took the class and passed it, you didn't have to study it again, they didn't change it, you were done! Albert Einstein said: "The hardest thing in the world to understand is the income tax." Financial guru Dave Ramsey is fond of saying that the tax code is so complicated that it can drive a Harvard graduate to fits of rage.

Congress passes laws that are effective this year, but not next year; laws that are effective the first Tuesday in February, but expire the third Thursday in November. It's maddening.

It's impossible for the average person to keep up. Of course, the way Congress intentionally writes the tax laws, it's impossible for any one person to comprehend them. We know those in Congress don't even necessarily read them. They've admitted it!

So, if taxes confuse you, it's no wonder. It's not your fault. My mission is to keep you from being an unwilling tax victim. So, sit up straight, take and deep breath, and exhale. Together we'll blow away this smoke of confusion.

I find that taxpayers can often be divided into three groups: Those who seek out a highly qualified professional to guide them through the haze of taxes, those who settle for the lowest price tax preparer, and those brave souls who do their own.

Before I became a CPA, I waffled between the first and last groups. I spent 15 years in the family business. There were good years and lean years. There were times when I sought out professional help one year and then tried to copy it on my own the next, completely unaware of the changes that had occurred.

Like my friend Todd. For years he prepared his own taxes using available software. You know the kind that says they have a "roadmap" or something to help you find all your deductions. Then one year he came to me and said: "Richard, I've already prepared my taxes, but I owe money. Would you see if you can do any better?" I analyzed his information, and without knowing what his result was before hand, we took advantage of a change in the Education Credits he was unaware of, and turned his balance due into a refund.

Then, there are those who know what they don't know and pay someone else to prepare their taxes. Within that group there are some of you who seek out the cheapest tax preparer they can find, thinking all tax preparers are created equal and are completely oblivious to the damage they can inflict. Most tax preparers charge based on the value they believe they bring, so, there's a reason they're the cheapest. What they don't know CAN hurt you.

You should be aware: Tax preparer <u>does not</u> equal tax advisor. Anyone with a pencil or a ten-year old computer can call themselves a tax preparer. No licensing, no training, no education required.

Do you know how the big chains get their tax preparers? Each winter they offer a one-night-a-week, six-week course on how to prepare your own tax return. They teach you what numbers go on what line of the Form 1040.

Then, they offer their best students a temporary, part-time, seasonal job as a tax preparer.

It's harder to become a barber!

You know what the problem with most CPAs is? They're BORING! But seriously, one of the biggest complaints I hear about other CPAs is that they aren't proactive in communicating with their clients about how to save on their taxes. Now don't get me wrong, most CPAs out there are smart, hard-working folks who would never knowingly do something wrong, but they just don't necessarily communicate with their clients unless the client comes up with the question.

What I hear from clients is that they want a CPA who comes up with some ideas on his own. They want someone who is willing to sit down and talk with them, explain things to them. They want a tax advisor, not just a tax preparer. Someone they can rely on to be up-to-date on the latest changes in tax laws, who will let them know about the changes and how those changes might affect them. So that's what I do.

It's not about putting numbers on a page. It's about a dialogue, a conversation between you and me. It's about the relationship.

That's why I wrote this book – not to help you become a tax expert, but to highlight the provisions most likely to impact you and to start the conversation. No matter how hard I try, I can't possibly know as much about your financial situation, whether business or personal, as you do. So, it is my hope that this book helps you to be better informed, and if something jumps out at you – something that might be applicable in your life – then you'll have a better idea of what question to ask.

What "Temporary" Tax Reform Means for You

The tax landscape has dramatically changed with the passage of the sweeping tax reform law commonly known as the Tax Cuts and Jobs Act. This legislation is the most comprehensive tax overhaul in over three decades. The Republicans bill it as creating fairness among taxpayers, while the Democrats decry it as folly.

There are new income tax rates and brackets, an increasing standard deduction and child credit, a suspension of the personal exemption, and limitations on the deduction of state and local taxes, among many other changes. There is also a brand-new deduction for non-corporate taxpayers with "qualified business income" from pass-throughs.

For businesses, the new law permanently reduces the corporate income tax rate to 21%, repeals the alternative minimum income tax, limits the deduction of business interest, and makes several changes involving depreciation.

Most of the changes went into effect January 1, 2018. **However, to keep the cost of the bill within Senate budget rules, the changes affecting individuals will expire after 2025. At that time, if no future Congress acts to extend or make permanent these changes, the provisions will sunset and the tax law will revert to its prior state.**

The number of **individual tax brackets** remains at seven, with a top individual rate of 37%. (Down from 39.6%.)

The new law will increase the **standard deduction** for individual taxpayers to $24,000 for married filing jointly, $18,000 for heads of households, and $12,000 for all others. The additional standard deduction for elderly and blind taxpayers is not changed.

All **personal exemptions** are repealed. The withholding rules and charts will be modified to reflect this.

Individuals who are owners in **pass-through entities**, such as partnerships, limited liability companies, S corporations, or sole proprietorships will be allowed to deduct 20% of "qualified business income". The new deduction will not be available for those in specified service industries such as accounting, health, law, consulting, athletics, financial services, brokerage services, or any business where the principal asset of the business is the reputation or skill of one or more of its employees.

A limitation on the deduction will be phased in based on W-2 wages above a threshold amount of taxable income, or with taxable income more than $157,500 or $315,000 in the case of a joint return.

For each qualified trade or business, the taxpayer will be allowed to deduct 20% of the qualified business income with respect to such trade or business.

Generally, the deduction is limited to 50% of the W-2 wages paid with respect to the business. Alternatively, a capital-intensive business may yield a higher benefit under a rule that takes into consideration 25% of wages paid plus a portion of the business's basis in tangible assets. However, if the taxpayer's income is below the threshold amount, the deductible amount for each qualified trade or business is equal to 20% of the qualified business income with respect to each trade or business.

The **child tax credit** will increase to $2,000 per qualifying child. The maximum refundable amount of the credit will be $1,400.

College Savings Plans (Sec. 529 Plans) will be able to distribute up to $10,000 for tuition and expenses at an elementary or secondary school.

Home **mortgage interest** deduction will be limited to the interest on acquisition indebtedness to $750,000, down from the current $1 million. Home equity loan interest will no longer be deductible.

Individuals will be limited to a $10,000 deduction for **state and local** income or property taxes.

All **miscellaneous itemized deductions** subject to the 2% floor (unreimbursed employee expenses, union dues, and tax preparation to name a few) have been repealed.

The threshold for the deduction of **medical expenses** will return to 7.5% of adjusted gross income.

The **Alternative Minimum Tax** (AMT) exemption amount will increase to $109,400 for married taxpayers filing a joint return (half that amount if filing separate) and $70,300 for all other individual taxpayers. The exemption and phase-out threshold amount will be indexed for inflation.

The **individual mandate** penalty for those taxpayers who do not obtain health insurance that provides at least minimum essential coverage, has been reduced to zero after 2018.

Changes to the Individual Income Tax Rates, Brackets, and Health Care Mandate

New Income Tax Rates and Brackets

The Internal Revenue Code provides four tax rate schedules for individuals based on filing status – i.e., single, married filing joint/surviving spouse, married filing separately, and head of household – each of which is divided into brackets in which income is progressively taxed at a higher rate. Under previous law, individuals were subject to seven tax rates: 10%, 15%, 25%, 28%, 33%, 35%, and 39.6%.

New law. For 2018 through 2025, seven slightly lower tax rates apply to individuals: 10%, 12%, 22%, 24%, 32%, 35%, and 37%.

Note: While these changes will lower the rates at many income levels, determining the overall impact on any particular individual or family will depend on a variety of other changes made by the new law, including increases in the standard deduction, loss of personal and dependency exemptions, a dollar limit on itemized deductions for state and local taxes, and changes to the child tax credit and the taxation of a child's unearned income, known as the Kiddie Tax.

Standard Deduction Increased

Taxpayers can reduce their adjusted gross income (AGI) by the greater of the standard deduction or the sum of their itemized deductions to determine their taxable income. Before the new law passed, the 2018 standard deductions were to be $6,500 for singles and married individuals filing separately, $9,550 for heads of households, and $13,000 for married couples filing jointly. The elderly or blind could claim additional standard deductions.

New law. For 2018 through 2025, the standard deduction is increased to $24,000 for those married couples filing a joint return, $18,000 for heads of households, and $12,000 for all other filers. Additional standard deductions are still available for the elderly and blind.

Personal Exemptions Suspended

Under former law, in addition the standard deduction, taxpayers were able to deduct personal exemptions from AGI to determine taxable income. Personal exemptions were allowed for the taxpayer, the taxpayer's spouse, and any dependents. The personal exemption amount for 2018 was scheduled to be $4,150, subject to a phase-out for high earners.

New law. For 2018 through 2025, the personal exemption is gone.

Capital Gains Provisions

An individual's net capital gains are taxed at maximum rates of 0%, 15%, or 20%.

Under former law, the 0% capital gains rate applied to income that would have otherwise been taxed at the 10% or 15% income tax rates; the 15% capital gains rate applied to income that would have otherwise been taxed at the 25%, 28%, 33% or 35% ordinary income tax rates; and the 20% capital gains rate applied to income more than those amounts.

New law. The current law maximum rates on net capital gains and qualified dividends remain the same. The new law retains the dollar amount breakpoints that existed under the former law but indexes them for inflation using C-CPI-U in tax years beginning in 2018.

For 2018, the 15% breakpoint is $77,200 for joint returns and surviving spouses (half this amount for married taxpayers filing separately), $51,700 for heads of household, $2,600 for trusts and estates, and $38,600 for other unmarried individuals. The 20% breakpoint is $479,000 for joint returns and surviving spouses (half this amount for married taxpayers filing separately), $452,400 for heads of household, $12,700 for trusts and estates, and $425,800 for other unmarried individuals.

Kiddie Tax Modified

The "Kiddie Tax" applies to a child if: (1) the child has not reached the age of 19 by the close of the tax year, or the child was a full-time student under the age of 24, and either of the child's parents was alive at such time; (2) the child's unearned income exceeds $2,100 (for 2018); and (3) the child did not file a joint return. Under former law, the Kiddie Tax provisions taxed the unearned income of a child at the parent's marginal tax rates if the parent's tax rates were higher than the child's. The remainder of a child's taxable income (i.e., earned income plus unearned income up to $2,100 (for 2018), less the child's standard deduction) at the child's rate.

New law. After 2017, the taxable income of a child attributable to earned income will be taxed under the rates for a single individual, and the taxable income of a child attributable to net unearned income will be taxed according to the brackets applicable to trusts and estates. See Appendix A.

Repeal of Obamacare Individual Mandate
Under current law, the Affordable Care Act (also known as the ACA or Obamacare) individuals who were not covered by a healthcare plan that provided at least minimum essential coverage were required to pay a "shared responsibility payment" with their federal tax return. Unless an exception applied, the penalty was imposed for any month that an individual did not have minimum essential coverage.

New law. Beginning January 2019, the amount of the individual shared responsibility payment is permanently reduced to zero.

Note: According to the Congressional Budget Office (CBO), reducing the penalty to zero would raise approximately $338 billion over the 10-year budgetary window. Because, when no longer penalized for not doing so, fewer people would obtain subsidized coverage.

Changes in Pass-through Income Deduction

New 20% Deduction for Qualified Business Income

Net income from sole proprietorships, partnerships, limited liability companies (LLCs), and S corporations is not subject to an entity level tax and instead is passed-through to the owners, or shareholders, on their respective income tax returns. Thus, the income is effectively subject to individual income tax rates.

New law. For years 2018 through 2025, a significant new tax deduction takes effect. It should provide a substantial tax benefit to individuals with "qualified business income" from a partnership, S Corporation, LLC, or sole proprietorship.

The deduction is 20% of your "qualified business income (QBI)" from a partnership, LLC, S corporation, or sole proprietorship, defined as the net amount of "qualified items of income, gain, deduction, and loss" with respect to your trade or business. The determination of qualified items of income, gain, deduction, and loss takes into account these items only to the extent included, or allowed, in the determination of taxable income for the year.

Example: In the current year a qualified business has $100,000 of ordinary income from inventory sales, and makes an expenditure of $25,000 that is required to be capitalized and amortized over 5 years under applicable tax rules. QBI is $100,000 - $5,000 (current year ordinary amortization deduction), or $95,000. QBI is reduced only by the amount deductible in determining taxable income for the year.

The business must be conducted within the U.S. to qualify, and specified investment related items are not included, e.g., capital gains or losses, dividends, and interest income (unless the interest is properly allocable to the business). The trade or business of being an employee does not qualify. Also, QBI does not include reasonable compensation received from an S Corporation, or a guaranteed payment received from a partnership for services provided to a partnership's business.

> *Example: Sam owns and operates an S Corporation which makes $300,000 before Sam's salary. Sam receives $100,000 in wages. Sam's deduction is 20% of $200,000, or $40,000.*

> *Example: Samantha is a partner who receives a guaranteed payment from a partnership. Her share of partnership profits equals $200,000 and she received $100,000 as a guaranteed payment. Samantha's deduction would be 20% of $200,000 or $40,000.*

The deduction is taken "below the line;" i.e., it reduces your taxable income, but not your adjusted gross income. But, it is available regardless of whether you itemize deductions or take the standard deduction. In general, the deduction cannot exceed 20% of the excess of your taxable income over net capital gain. If QBI is less than zero, it is treated as a loss from a qualified business in the following year.

> *Example: Taxpayer has QBI of $20,000 from qualified business A and a qualified business loss of $50,000 from qualified business B in year one. Taxpayer is not permitted a deduction for year 1 and has a carryover qualified business loss of $30,000 to year 2.*

> *In year 2, taxpayer has QBI of $20,000 from qualified business A and QBI of $50,000 from qualified business B. To determine the deduction for year 2, taxpayer reduces the 20% deductible amount determined for the QBI of $70,000 from qualified business A and B by 20% of the $30,000 carryover qualified business loss.*

22

Rules are in place to deter high income taxpayers from attempting to convert wages, or other compensation, for personal services into income eligible for the deduction.

For taxpayers with taxable income above $157,500 ($315,000 for joint filers), an exclusion from QBI of income from "specified service" trades or businesses is phased in. These are trades or businesses involving the performance of services in the fields of health, law, consulting, athletics, accounting, financial or brokerage services, or where the principal asset is the reputation or skill of one or more employees or owners.

Here's how the phase-in works: If your taxable income is at least $50,000 above the threshold -- i.e., $207,500 ($157,000 + $50,000) -- all the net income from the specified service trade or business is excluded from QBI. (Joint filers would use an amount $100,000 above the $315,000 threshold, i.e., $415,000.) If your taxable income is between $157,500 and $207,500, you would exclude only that percentage of income derived from a fraction -- the numerator of which is the excess of taxable income over $157,500, and the denominator of which is $50,000. So, for example, if taxable income is $167,500 ($10,000 above $157,500), only 20% of the specified service income would be excluded from QBI ($10,000/$50,000). (For joint filers, the same operation would apply using the $315,000 threshold, and a $100,000 phase-out range.)

Additionally, for taxpayers with taxable income more than the above thresholds, a limitation on the amount of the deduction is phased in based either on wages paid or wages paid plus a capital element.

Here's how it works: If your taxable income is at least $50,000 above the threshold -- i.e., $207,500 ($157,500 + $50,000) -- your deduction for QBI cannot exceed the greater of (1) 50% of your allocable share of the W-2 wages paid with respect to the qualified trade or business, or (2) the sum of 25% of such wages plus 2.5% of the unadjusted basis immediately after acquisition of qualified tangible depreciable property used in the business (including real estate). So, if you're QBI were $100,000, leading to a deduction of $20,000 (20% of $100,000), but the greater of (1) or (2) above were only $16,000, your deduction would be limited to $16,000 -- i.e., it would be reduced by $4,000. And if your taxable income were between $157,500 and $207,500 you would only receive a pro rata percentage of the $4,000 reduction. (For joint filers, the same operations would apply using the $315,000 threshold, and a $100,000 phaseout range.)

Other limitations may apply in certain circumstances; e.g., for taxpayers with qualified cooperative dividends, qualified real estate investment trust (REIT) dividends, or income from publicly traded partnerships.

Changes to Loss Provisions

New Limitations on "Excess Business Loss"

In general, the passive activity loss rules limit deductions and credits from passive trade or business activities. The passive loss rules apply to individuals, estates and trusts, and closely held corporations. A passive activity for this purpose is a trade or business activity in which the taxpayer owns an interest but does not materially participate. "Material participation" means that the taxpayer is involved in the operation of the activity on a basis that is regular, continuous, and substantial. Deductions attributable to passive activities, to the extent they exceed income from passive activities, generally may not be deducted against other income and are carried forward and treated as deductions and credits from passive activities in the next year.

New law. For 2018 through 2025, excess business losses are not allowed for the tax year, but are instead carried forward and treated as part of the taxpayer's net operating loss (NOL) carryforward in subsequent tax years. This limitation applies after the application of the passive loss rules described above.

An excess business loss for the tax year is the excess of aggregate deductions over income or gain attributable to the taxpayer's trades and businesses plus a threshold amount. The threshold amount for a tax year is $500,000 for married individuals filing jointly, and $250,000 for other individuals.

In the case of a partnership or S Corporation, the provision applies at the partner or shareholder level. Each partner's or shareholder's share of items of income, gain, deduction, or loss of the partnership or S corporation is taken into account in applying the above limitation for the tax year of the partner or shareholder.

Personal Casualty and Theft Loss Deduction Suspended

Under prior law, individuals could claim an itemized deduction for uncompensated personal casualty losses, including those arising from fire, storm, shipwreck, or other casualty, or from theft.

New law. For 2018 through 2025, the personal casualty and theft loss deduction is suspended, except for personal casualty losses incurred in a federally declared disaster area. However, where a taxpayer has personal casualty gains, the law suspension doesn't apply to the extent that such loss doesn't exceed the gain.

Changes to Personal Deductions, Exclusions and Credits

Mortgage Interest Deduction limited

Under former law, a taxpayer could deduct interest on up to a total of $1 million of mortgage debt used to acquire your principal residence and a second home, i.e., acquisition debt. For married taxpayers filing separately, the limit was $500,000. You could also deduct interest on home equity debt -- i.e., other debt secured by the qualifying homes. Qualifying home equity debt was limited to the lesser of $100,000 ($50,000 for married taxpayers filing separately), of the taxpayer's equity in the home, or homes. The funds obtained via a home equity loan did not have to be used to acquire or improve the homes. So, you could use home equity debt to pay for education, travel, healthcare, etc.

New law. For 2018 through 2025, the deduction for interest on home equity loans is suspended, and the deduction for mortgage interest is limited to an underlying loan of up to $750,000 ($375,000 for married taxpayers filing separately).

Note: The new lower limit doesn't apply to any acquisition indebtedness incurred before December 15, 2017.

Note: The $1 million/$500,000 limitations continue to apply to taxpayers who refinance existing qualified residence debt that was incurred before December 15, 2017, so long as the indebtedness resulting from the refinancing doesn't exceed the amount of the refinanced debt.

State and Local Tax Deduction Limited

Under former law, a taxpayer was permitted to claim several types of taxes paid at the state and local level, including real and personal property taxes, income taxes, and/or sales taxes, as an itemized deduction even if they were not business related. Taxpayers could elect to deduct state and local general sales taxes in lieu of state and local income taxes.

New law. For 2018 through 2025, a taxpayer is limited to an itemized deduction of $10,000 ($5,000 for marrieds filing separate returns) for the aggregate of (a) state and local property taxes not paid or accrued in carrying on a trade or business, and (b) state and local income taxes, war profits, and excess profits taxes (or sales taxes in lieu of income taxes) paid in the year. Foreign real property taxes may not be deducted.

State, local, and foreign property taxes, and state and local sales taxes, are fully deductible only when paid or accrued in carrying on a trade or business or other activity conducted for the production of income.

Miscellaneous Itemized Deductions Suspended
Under former law, individuals could deduct certain miscellaneous itemized deductions to the extent that they exceeded, in the aggregate, 2% of the taxpayer's AGI.

New law. For 2018 through 2025, the deduction for miscellaneous itemized deductions that are subject to the 2% floor is suspended.

Certain miscellaneous itemized deductions were permanently repealed, including:
- appraisal fees for a casualty loss or charitable contribution;
- casualty and theft losses from property used in performing services as an employee;
- clerical help and office rent in caring for investments;
- depreciation on home computers used for investments;
- excess deductions allowed a beneficiary on termination of an estate or trust;
- fees to collect interest and dividends;
- hobby expenses, but generally not more than hobby income;
- indirect miscellaneous deductions from pass-through entities;
- investment fees and expenses;
- loss on deposits in an insolvent or bankrupt financial institution;
- loss on traditional IRAs or Roth IRAs, when all amounts have been distributed;
- repayments of income;

- safe deposit box rental fees, except for storing jewelry and other personal effects;
- service charges on dividend reinvestment plans;
- trustee's fees for an IRA, if separately billed and paid;
- tax preparation expenses; and
- unreimbursed expenses of an employee.

Medical Expense Deduction Threshold Reduced
An itemized deduction is allowed for medical expenses paid during the year which exceed a threshold amount. Medical expenses include payments for the medical care of the taxpayer, the taxpayer's spouse, and the taxpayer's dependents. Any insurance or other reimbursements must reduce the payment amounts before the threshold is applied. Under former law the threshold was generally 10% of AGI.

New law. For 2017 and 2018, the threshold on medical expense deductions is temporarily reduced to 7.5%.

Charitable Contribution Deduction Limit Increased
An individual's charitable contribution deduction is limited to prescribed percentages of the taxpayer's "contribution base." Under former law, the percentages were 50%, 30%, or 20%, depending on the type of organization to which the contribution was made, whether the contribution was made "to" or merely "for the use of" the recipient organization, and whether the contribution consisted of capital gain property. The 50% limitation applied to public charities and certain private organizations.

No deduction is allowed for contributions of $250 or more, unless the donor substantiates the contribution by a contemporaneous written acknowledgment from the recipient organization.

New law. For 2018 through 2025, the 50% limitation for cash contributions to public charities and certain private foundations is increased to 60%. Contributions exceeding the 60% limitation are generally allowed to be carried forward and deducted for up to 5 years, subject to the later year's ceiling.

No Deduction for College Athletic Seating Rights
Under former law, special rules applied to certain payments to institutions of higher education in exchange for which the payor receive the right to

purchase tickets or seating at an athletic event. The payor could treat 80% of a payment as a charitable contribution where the amount was paid to or for the benefit of an institution of higher education and such amount would be allowable as a charitable deduction but for the fact that the taxpayer receives (directly or indirectly) the right to purchase tickets for seating at an athletic event.

New law. For contributions made after 2017, no charitable deduction is allowed for any payment to an institution of higher education in exchange for which the payor receives the right to purchase tickets or seating at an athletic event.

Alimony Deduction Suspended
Under former law, alimony and separate maintenance payments were deductible by the payor spouse and includable in income by the recipient spouse.

New law. For any divorce or separation agreement executed after December 31, 2018, or executed before that date but modified after it, alimony and separate maintenance payments are not deductible by the payor spouse and are not includable in the income of the payee spouse.

Note: It's important to emphasize that the current rules continue to apply to already existing divorces and separations, as well as divorces and separations that are executed before 2019.

Moving Expense Deduction Suspended
A deduction for moving expenses incurred relating to starting a new job could be taken, under former law, by a taxpayer if the new workplace was at least 50 miles further from the taxpayer's former residence than the former place of work.

New law. For 2018 through 2025, the deduction for moving expenses is suspended, except for members of the Armed Forces on active duty who moved pursuant to a military order and incident to a permanent change of station.

Exclusion for Moving Expense Reimbursements Suspended
Under former law, qualified moving expense reimbursements were excluded from an employee's gross income and from his or her wages for

employment tax purposes. This included money received from an employer as payment for, or reimbursement of, expenses which would be deductible as moving expenses if paid or incurred directly by the employee.

New law. For 2018 through 2025, the exclusion for qualified moving expense reimbursements is suspended, except for members of the Armed Forces on active duty, and their spouses and dependents, who moved pursuant to a military order and incident to a permanent change of station.

Child Tax Credit Increased
Under former law, a child tax credit was available up to $1,000 per qualifying child under the age of 17. The credit was phased out when adjusted gross income exceeded $75,000 for single filers, $110,000 for married filers, and $55,000 for married individuals filing separately. To the extent that the credit exceeded a taxpayer's liability, a taxpayer was eligible for a refundable credit equal to 15% of earned income more than $3,000.

New law. For 2018 through 2025, the child tax credit is increased to $2,000. The income levels at which the credit phases out are increased to $400,000 for married taxpayers filing jointly, and $200,000 for all other taxpayers. In addition, a $500 nonrefundable credit is provided for certain non-child dependents. The amount of the credit that is refundable is increased to $1,400 per qualifying child, up to the base $2,000 credit. The earned income threshold for the refundable portion of the credit is decreased from $3,000 to $2,500. No credit will be allowed to a taxpayer with respect to any qualifying child unless the taxpayer provides the child's Social Security number.

Changes to Depreciation, Expensing, and Capitalization

Temporary 100% Cost Recovery of Qualifying Business Assets

Under former law, an additional first-year bonus depreciation deduction of 50% of the adjusted basis of qualified property was allowed if the original use began with the taxpayer and the property was placed in service before January 1, 2020. The 50% allowance was phased down for property placed in service after December 31, 2017.

New law. A 100% first-year deduction for the adjusted basis is allowed for qualified property acquired and placed in service after September 27, 2017, and before January 1, 2023. Thus, the phase-down of the 50% allowance for property placed in service after December 31, 2017 is repealed. The additional first-year depreciation deduction is allowed for new and used property.

Note: The Act refers to the new 100% depreciation deduction in the placed-in-service year as "100% expensing," but the tax break should not be confused with expensing under Code Sec. 179, which is subject to entirely separate rules.

In later years, the first-year bonus depreciation deduction phases down as follows:
- 80% for property placed in service during calendar year 2023,
- 60% for property placed in service during calendar year 2024,
- 40% for property placed in service during calendar year 2025,
- 20% for property placed in service during calendar year 2026.

Increased Code Sec. 179 Expensing

A taxpayer may, subject to limitations, elect under Code Sec. 179 to deduct, or expense, the cost of qualifying property, rather than to recover such costs through depreciation. Under former law, the maximum amount a taxpayer could expense was $500,000 of the cost of qualifying property placed in service for the tax year. The $500,000 amount was reduced by the amount by which the cost of qualifying property placed in service during the tax year exceeds $2 million.

In general, qualifying property is defined as depreciable tangible personal property that is purchased for use in the active conduct of a trade or business, and includes off-the-shelf computer software and qualified real property -- i.e., qualified leasehold improvement property, qualified restaurant property, and qualified retail improvement property.

Passenger automobiles subject to the luxury automobile limitations are eligible for Code Sec. 179 expensing only to the extent of the luxury automobile dollar limitations. For sport-utility vehicles above the 6,000-pound weight rating and not more than the 14,000-pound weight rating, the maximum cost that may be expensed for any tax year under Code Sec. 179 is $25,000.

New law. For property placed in service in tax years beginning after December 31, 2017, the maximum amount a taxpayer may expense under Code Sec. 179 is increased to $1 million, and the phase-out threshold amount is increased to $2.5 million. For tax years beginning after 2018, these amounts are indexed for inflation.

The definition of Code Sec. 179 property is expanded to include certain depreciable tangible personal property used predominantly to furnish lodging or in connection with furnished lodging. The definition of "qualified real property" eligible for Code Sec. 179 expensing is also expanded to include the following improvements to nonresidential real property after the date such property was first placed in service: roofs, heating, ventilation and air-conditioning property, fire protection and alarm systems, and security systems.

Luxury Automobile Limitations Increased

The depreciation deduction and Code Sec. 179 expensing with respect to certain passenger autos is limited. Under former law, for passenger automobiles placed in service in 2017, the maximum amount of allowable depreciation deduction is $3,160 for the year in which the vehicle is placed in service, $5,100 for the second year, $3,050 for the third year, and $1,875 for the fourth and later years in the recovery period.

For passenger automobiles eligible for the additional first-year depreciation allowance in 2017, the first-year limitation is increased by an additional $8,000. This amount is phased down from $8,000 by $1,600 per calendar year beginning in 2018. Thus, the additional first-year depreciation allowance available in 2018 is $6,400.

Special rules also apply to listed property, such as any passenger auto or other property used as a means of transportation, any property of a type generally used for purposes of entertainment, recreation, or amusement, and, under former law, any computer or peripheral equipment.

New law. For passenger automobiles placed in service after December 31, 2017, for which the additional first-year depreciation deduction is not claimed, the maximum amount of allowable depreciation is increased to $10,000 for the year in which the vehicle is placed in service, $16,000 for the second year, $9,600 for the third year, and $5,760 for the fourth and later years in the recovery period.

Computer and peripheral equipment are removed from the definition of listed property, and so, aren't subject to the heightened substantiation requirements that apply to listed property.

Real Property Recovery Period is Shortened
The cost recovery periods for nonresidential real property and residential rental property are 39 years and 27.5 years, respectively. The straight-line depreciation method and mid-month convention are required for such real property.

Under former law, qualified leasehold improvement property was an interior building improvement to nonresidential real property, by a landlord, tenant or subtenant, that was placed in service more than 3 years after the building is placed in service and that meets other requirements. Qualified restaurant property was a building improvement in a building in which more than 50% of the building's square footage was devoted to the preparation of, and seating for, on-premises consumption of prepared meals. Qualified retail improvement property was an interior improvement to retail space that was placed in service more than 3 years after the date the building was first placed in service and that meets other requirements.

Qualified improvement property is any improvement to an interior portion of a building that is nonresidential real property if such improvement is placed in service after the date such building was first placed in service. Qualified improvement property does not include any improvement for which the expenditure is attributable to the enlargement of the building, any elevator or escalator, or the internal structural framework of the building.

New law. For property placed in service after December 31, 2017, the separate definitions of qualified leasehold improvement, qualified restaurant, and qualified retail improvement property are eliminated. A general 15-year recovery period and straight-line depreciation are provided for qualified improvement property.

Farming Equipment Recovery Period is Shortened

Under former law, depreciable assets used in agriculture activities that are assigned a recovery period of 7 years include: machinery and equipment; grain bins; and fences that are used in the production of crops or plants, vines, trees, livestock, dairies, nurseries, greenhouses, sod farms, mushroom cellars, cranberry bogs, aviaries, fur firms, and animal husbandry and horticulture services. Cotton ginning assets are also assigned a recovery period of 7 years, while land improvements such as drainage facilities, paved lots, and water wells are assigned a recovery period of 15 years.

Any property used in a farming business is subject to the 150% declining balance method.

New law. For property placed in service after December 31, 2017, the depreciation period is shortened from 7 to 5 years for any machinery or equipment used in a farming business (other than any grain bin, cotton ginning asset, fence, or other land improvement), the original use of which commences with the taxpayer.

In addition, the required use of the 150% declining balance depreciation method for farm machinery and equipment is repealed. The 150% declining balance method continues to apply to any 15-year or 20-year property used in the farming business.

Changes in Business Deductions

Business Interest Deduction Limited

Subject to some limitations, interest paid or accrued by a business is generally deductible in the computation of taxable income. For a non-corporate taxpayer, the deduction for interest on debt that is allocable to property held for investment (investment interest) is limited to the taxpayer's net investment income for the tax year.

A deduction for interest may be disallowed for a corporation if the payor's debt to equity ratio exceeds 1.5 to 1 and the payor's net interest expense exceeds 50% of its adjusted taxable income (generally, taxable income computed without regard to the deductions for net interest expense, net operating losses, domestic production activities, depreciation, amortization, and depletion).

New law. For tax years beginning after December 31, 2017, every business, regardless of its form, is generally subject to a disallowance of an interest expense deduction in excess of 30% of the business's adjusted taxable income. The net interest expense disallowance is determined at the tax filer level. However, a special rule applies to pass-through entities, which requires the determination to be made at the entity level, for example, at the partnership level instead of the partner level.

For tax years beginning after December 31, 2017 and before January 1, 2022, adjusted taxable income is computed without regard to deductions allowable for depreciation, amortization, or depletion.

The amount of any business interest not allowed as a deduction for any taxable year is treated as a business interest paid or accrued in the succeeding taxable year. Business interest may be carried forward indefinitely, subject to certain restrictions applicable to partnerships.

An exemption from these rules applies for taxpayers with average annual gross receipts for the three-tax year period ending with the prior tax year that do not exceed $25 million. Real property trades or businesses can elect out of the provision if they use the Alternative Depreciation System (ADS) to depreciate applicable real property used in a trade or business. Farming businesses can also elect out if they use ADS to depreciate any property used in the farming business with the recovery period of 10 years or more. An exception from the limitation on the business interest deduction is also provided for floor plan financing (i.e., financing for the acquisition of motor vehicles, boats or farm machinery for sale or lease and secured by such inventory).

The limit on the amount allowed as a deduction for business interest is increased by a partner's distributive share of the partnership's excess taxable income. The excess taxable income for any partnership is the amount which bears the same ratio to the partnership's adjusted taxable income as the excess (if any) of 30% of the adjusted taxable income of the partnership over the amount (if any) by which the business interest of the partnership, reduced by floor plan financing interest, exceeds the business interest income of the partnership bears to 30% of the adjusted taxable income of the partnership. As a result, a partner of a partnership can deduct additional interest expense the partner may have paid or incurred to the extent the partnership could have deducted more business interest. Excess taxable income is allocated in the same manner as non-separately stated income and loss. Similar rules apply to S corporations.

In the case of a partnership, any business interest that is not allowed as a deduction to the partnership for the tax year is allocated to each partner in the same manner as non-separately stated taxable income or loss of the partnership. The partner may deduct its share of the partnership's excess business interest in the future year, but only against excess taxable income attributed to the partner by the partnership activities which gave rise to the excess business interest carryforward. Any such deduction requires a corresponding reduction in excess taxable income. In addition, when excess business interest is allocated to a partner, the partner's basis in its partnership interest is reduced (but not below zero) by the amount of such allocation, even though the carryforward does not give rise to a partner deduction in the year of the basis reduction. However, the partner's deduction in a future year for interest carryforward does not reduce the partner's basis in the partnership interest.

Net Operating Loss Deduction Modified
Under former law, a net operating loss (NOL) may generally be carried back two years and carried over 20 years to offset taxable income in such years. However, different carryback periods apply with respect to NOLs arising in different circumstances. For example, extended carryback periods are allowed for NOLs attributable to specified liability losses in certain casualty and disaster losses.

New law. For NOLs arising in tax years ending after December 31, 2017, the two-year carryback and the special carryback provisions are repealed, but a two-year carryback applies in the case of certain losses incurred in the trade or business of farming.

For losses arising in tax years beginning after December 31, 2017, the NOL deduction is limited to 80% of taxable income (determined without regard to the deduction). Carryovers to other years are adjusted to take account of this limitation, and, except as provided below, NOLs can be carried forward indefinitely.

NOLs of property and casualty insurance companies can be carried back two years and carried over 20 years to offset 100% of taxable income in such years.

Like-kind Exchange Treatment Limited
The like-kind exchange rule provides that no gain or loss is recognized to the extent that property -- which included a wide range of property from real estate to tangible personal property -- held for productive use in the taxpayer's trade or business, or property held for investment purposes, is exchanged for property of a like kind that also is held for productive use in a trade or business or for investment.

New law. Generally effective for transfers after December 31, 2017, the rule allowing the deferral of gain on like-kind exchanges is modified to allow for like-kind exchanges only with respect to real property that is not held primarily for sale. However, under a transition rule, the former like-kind exchange rules apply to exchanges of personal property if the taxpayer has either disposed of the relinquished property or acquired the replacement property on or before December 31, 2017.

Meals and Entertainment Deduction Limited
Under current law, a taxpayer may deduct up to 50% of the cost of meals and entertainment. Housing and meals provided for the convenience of the employer on the business premises of the employer are excluded from the employee's gross income.

New law. Deductions for entertainment expenses are disallowed for amounts incurred or paid after December 31, 2017, eliminating the subjective determination of whether such expenses are sufficiently business related. The current 50% limit on the deductibility of business meals is expanded to meals provided through an in-house cafeteria or otherwise on the premises of the employer.

For tax years beginning after December 31, 2025, an employer's deduction for expenses associated with meals provided for the convenience of the employer on the employer's business premises, or provided on or near the employer's business premises through an employer-operated facility that meets certain requirements will be disallowed.

Sexual Harassment Settlement Deduction Disallowed
A taxpayer is generally allowed to deduct ordinary and necessary expenses paid or incurred in carrying on any trade or business. Certain exceptions include illegal bribes, illegal kickbacks, other illegal payments, certain lobbying and political expenses, any fine or similar penalty paid to a government for the violation of any law, and two-thirds of treble damage payments under the antitrust laws.

New law. Effective for amounts paid or incurred after December 22, 2017, no deduction is allowed for any settlement, payout, or attorney fees related to sexual harassment or sexual abuse if such payments are subject to a non-disclosure agreement.

Family and Medical Leave Credit Added
Previously, no credit was provided to employers for compensation paid to employees while on leave.

New law. For wages paid in tax years beginning after December 31, 2017, but not beginning before December 31, 2019, businesses will be allowed to claim a general business credit equal to 12.5% of the amount of wages paid to qualifying employees during any period in which such employees are on family and medical leave (FMLA) if the rate of payment is 50% of the wages normally paid to an employee. The credit is increased by 0.25 percentage points (but not above 25%) for each percentage point by which the rate of payment exceeds 50%. To qualify for the credit, all qualifying full-time employees must be given at least two weeks of annual paid family and medical leave (all less than full-time qualifying employees must be given a commensurate amount of leave on a pro rata basis).

Changes to Tax-Preferred Accounts

Expanded Use of 529 Account Funds

Under former law, Code Sec. 529 college savings account funds could only be used for qualified higher education expenses. If funds were withdrawn from the account for other purposes, each withdrawal was treated as containing a pro rata portion of earnings and principal. The earnings portion of a nonqualified withdrawal was taxable as ordinary income and subject to a 10% penalty unless an exception applied.

"Qualified higher education expenses" included tuition, fees, books, supplies, and required equipment, as well as reasonable room and board if the student was enrolled at least half-time. Eligible schools included colleges, universities, vocational schools, or other postsecondary schools eligible to participate in a student aid program of the Department of Education. This included nearly all accredited public, nonprofit, and for-profit postsecondary institutions.

New law. For distributions after 2017, "qualified higher education expenses" included tuition at an elementary or secondary public, private, or religious school, up to a $10,000 limit per year.

ABLE Account Changes

Individuals with disabilities and their families could fund a tax preferred savings account to pay for "qualified" disability related expenses using ABLE accounts. Contributions may be made by parents, family members, the person with a disability, or others. Under former law, the annual limitation on contributions is the amount of the annual gift-tax exemption ($15,000 in 2018).

New law. For 2018 through 2025, the contribution limitation to ABLE accounts with respect to contributions made by the designated beneficiary (the person with a disability) is increased, and other changes are in effect as described below. After the overall limitation on contributions is reached (the annual gift-tax exemption amount), an ABLE account's designated beneficiary can contribute an additional amount, up to the lesser of the federal poverty line for a one-person household or the individual's compensation for the year.

Additionally, the designated beneficiary of an ABLE account can claim the saver's credit for contributions made to his or her ABLE account.

The designated beneficiary, or person acting on the beneficiary's behalf, must maintain adequate records for ensuring compliance with the above limitations.

For distributions after December 22, 2017, amounts from qualified tuition programs (QTPs, also known as 529 accounts) can be rolled over to an ABLE account without penalty, provided that the ABLE account is owned by the designated beneficiary of that 529 account, or a member of such designated beneficiary's family. Such rolled over amounts are counted towards the overall limitation on amounts that can be contributed to an ABLE account within a tax year, and any amount rolled over more than this limitation is includable in the gross income of the distributee.

IRA Recharacterization Rules Repealed
Under former law, if an individual contributed to either a traditional or Roth IRA, the individual could recharacterize the contribution as a contribution to the other type of IRA by making a trustee-to-trustee transfer to the other type of IRA before the due date for the individual's income tax return for that year. In the case of a recharacterization, the contribution was treated as having been made to the transferee IRA as of the date of the original contribution. Both regular contributions and conversion contributions to a Roth IRA could be recharacterize as having been made to a traditional IRA.

New law. Beginning in 2018, the rule that allows a contribution to one type of IRA to be recharacterized as a contribution to the other type of IRA does not apply to a conversion contribution to a Roth IRA. Thus, recharacterization cannot be used to unwind a Roth conversion.

Changes to Corporate Taxes

Corporate Tax Rates Reduced

Under former law, corporations were subject to graduated rates of 15% for taxable income up to $50,000, 25% (for taxable income of $50,001-$75,000), 34% (for taxable income of $75,001-$10 million), and 35% (for taxable income over $10 million). Personal service corporations pay tax on their entire taxable income at the rate of 35%.

New law. For tax years beginning after December 31, 2017, the corporate tax rate is a flat 21% rate.

Alternative Minimum Tax Repealed

Under former law, the corporate alternative minimum tax (AMT) was 20%, with an exemption amount up to $40,000. Corporations with average gross receipts of less than $7.5 million for the preceding three tax years are exempt from the AMT. The exemption amount phases out starting at $150,000 of alternative minimum taxable income.

New law. For tax years beginning after December 31, 2017, the corporate AMT is repealed.

For tax years beginning after 2017 and before 2022, the AMT credit is refundable and can offset regular tax liability in an amount equal to 50% (100% for tax years beginning before 2022) of the excess of the minimum tax credit for the tax year over the amount of the credit allowable for the year against regular tax liability. Accordingly, the full amount of the minimum tax credit will be allowed in tax years beginning before 2022.

Appendix A

Single Individuals

If taxable income is:	Then, income tax equals:
Not over $9,525	10% of the taxable income
Over $9,525, but not over $38,700	$952.50, plus 12% of the excess over $9,525
Over $38,700, but not over $82,500	$4,453.50, plus 22% of the excess over $38,700
Over $82,500, but not over $157,500	$14,089.50, plus 24% of the excess over $82,500
Over $157,500, but not over $200,000	$32,089.50, plus 32% of the excess over $157,500
Over $200,000, but not over $500,000	$45,689.50, plus 35% of the excess over $200,000
Over $500,000	$150,689.50, plus 37% of the excess over $500,000

Heads of Households

If taxable income is:	Then, income tax equals:
Not over $13,600	10% of the taxable income
Over $13,600, but not over $51,800	$1,360, plus 12% of the excess over $13,600
Over $51,800, but not over $82,500	$5,944, plus 22% of the excess over $51,800
Over $82,500, but not over $157,500	$12,698, plus 24% of the excess over $82,500
Over $157,500, but not over $200,000	$30,698, plus 32% of the excess over $157,500
Over $200,000, but not over $500,000	$44,298, plus 35% of the excess over $200,00
Over $500,000	$149,298, plus 37% of the excess over $500,000

Married individuals filing joint returns and surviving spouses

If taxable income is:	Then, income tax equals:
Not over $19,050	10% of the taxable income
Over $19,050, but not over $77,400	$1,905, plus 12% of the excess over $19,050
Over $77,400, but not over $165,000	$8,907, plus 22% of the excess over $77,400
Over $165,000, but not over $315,000	$28,179, plus 24% of the excess over $165,000
Over $315,000, but not over $400,000	$64,179, plus 32% of the excess over $315,000
Over $400,000, but not over $600,000	$91,379, plus 35% of the excess over $400,000
Over $600,000	$161,379, plus 37% of the excess over $600,000

Married individuals filing separate returns

If taxable income is:	Then, income tax equals:
Not over $9,525	10% of the taxable income
Over $9,525, but not over $38,700	$952.50, plus 12% of the excess over $9.525
Over $38,700, but not over $82,500	$4,453.50, plus 22% of the excess over $38,700
Over $82,500, but not over $157,500	$14,089.50, plus 24% of the excess over $82,500
Over $157,500, but not over $200,000	$32,089.50, plus 32% of the excess over $157,500
Over $200,000, but not over $300,000	$45,689.50, plus 35% of the excess over $200,000
Over $300,000	$80,689.50, plus 37% of the excess over $300,000

Estates and trusts

If taxable income is:	Then, income tax equals:
Not over $2,550	10% of the taxable income
Over $2,550, but not over $9,150	$255, plus 24% of the excess over $2,550
Over $9,150, but not over $12,500	$1,839, plus 35% of the excess over $9,150
Over $12,500	$3,011.50, plus 37% of the excess over $12,500